LOST LINES OF WALES
THE HEADS OF THE VALLEYS LINE

GEOFFREY LLOYD

GRAFFEG

CONTENTS

This series of books aims to revive nostalgic memories of some of the more interesting and scenic railways which served the people of Wales. This volume recalls the heyday of one of the most scenic, the Merthyr, Tredegar & Abergavenny Railway, the MT&A.

The line followed a rather tortuous route that tested the limits of the motive power of the day, clinging tenuously to the sides of the Clydach Gorge, climbing steep gradients, crossing rivers, and finally ending in a long six-mile descent into the important industrial town of Merthyr. Freight trains would quite literally flog themselves up steep inclines whilst wagon brakes were applied to trains travelling in the opposite direction. The line was one of the most heavily engineered in south Wales, its inclines so steep that banking engines were needed in both directions, hence the large number of locomotives allocated to Abergavenny engine shed.

The line carried a considerable volume of traffic from the time it was opened until shortly after World War I. Initially it was minerals and raw materials to the ironworks around the Merthyr area then completed products out to markets around the world. Due to the abundance of Welsh steam coal especially anthracite, coal traffic was particularly heavy especially during WW I when long coal trains known as 'Jellicoe Specials', so named after Admiral of the Fleet, Lord Jellicoe, would head northwards filled with the bountiful supplies to be found in the south Wales coalfields. These would travel via the MT&A and Abergavenny to the far north of Scotland to supply the Royal Navy's Grand Fleet at Scapa Flow.

Passenger traffic was especially busy throughout the summer months with many day-trippers travelling to the resorts of south Wales and further afield to the north Wales coastal resorts and even Blackpool. There was an extensive colliers' train service not shown in public timetables, some as many as 20 coaches long taking workmen to the many pits 'down the valley'.

In common with many other closed lines around the country, no effort seemed to have been made to reopen any part of this lost line. This is a shame as for many years following closure and the lifting of the track, steps could have been taken to retain, at least in part, some of the line as a heritage railway although the cost of maintaining bridges, tunnels and viaducts would ultimately have become prohibitively expensive; the estimated saving to British Railways when it closed was some £60,000 annually. Ironically, in the 1950s sections of track were renewed prior to closure and the Clydach section won best track length for several years running, as did Abergavenny in 1955. However, most of the original track bed can still be seen and much of this is now a dedicated walkway or cycle track. Along the way some of the old stations have been retained and are now private dwellings. Some of the original signage and platforms are also still visible so one can walk or cycle the route and and get some sense of what it was like in its heyday.

INTRODUCTION

This railway line running 24 ½ miles due west from Abergavenny to Merthyr was built to capitalise on the growing industrial base in the area and later to bring passengers to the important market town of Abergavenny, immortalised by the singer Marty Wilde MBE in his 1968 hit single. Abergavenny, which is known as the 'Gateway to Wales', always seemed to have an air of prosperity about it and the inclusion of three railway stations, Abergavenny Junction, Brecon Road and Monmouth Road, further added to its importance. In its heyday, over 1,000 people worked for the railways, which made it one of the largest employers in the area. A number of these railway servants tragically laid down their lives for their country in the Great War and a plaque to their memory is proudly displayed in the entrance to the Market Hall. Today the town's only station is just known as Abergavenny, and is located on the busy north-west route from Cardiff to Crewe.

Dr Richard Beeching's infamous report, *The Reshaping of British Railways,* published in 1963, led to large-scale closures of lines and stations throughout the UK and Wales suffered its fair share of these as a result. Though some have re-opened many have not, and their passing is still mourned. However, we cannot blame Dr Beeching for the demise of this line, which finally gave up the struggle for survival on 4th January 1958 following falling revenues from freight traffic, declining passenger numbers and increasing operational costs. The last train over the whole length of the line from Abergavenny to Merthyr, on 5th January 1958, the day after public sevices ended, was a railtour organised by the Stephenson Locomotive Society and hauled appropriately by a pair of surviving ex-LNWR locomotives. The line between Abergavenny Brecon Road goods yard and Abergavenny Junction remained open for goods traffic until 4th April 1971 and was the last section of the Merthyr, Tredegar & Abergavenny line to close.

The precursor to this line was a number of tramroads some of which were built and later acquired by one of the ironmasters, Crawshay Bailey. These were built to transport raw materials to the Nantyglo area, where he had a number of ironworks, and to move completed goods out to markets worldwide. Bailey was an industrialist and railway pioneer who had acquired the Nantyglo Works in 1813 and whose early enthusiasm for steam locomotives was immortalised in the folk song about *Crawshay Bailey's engine*. The impact that he had at the time and the legacy that he left throughout Wales still exists today.

Crawshay Bailey was not a native Welshman, but he certainly left his mark on the Welsh landscape. He grew up in Yorkshire but left at the age of twelve to join with his elder brother Joseph and learn the iron trade from their uncle, Richard Crawshay. On their uncle's death, legacies were left to them to enable the purchase of the Nantyglo Ironworks and subsequently the Beaufort Ironworks. Between them they became the greatest ironworks in the world.

In 1822 Bailey opened a 5 ½ mile plateway known as Bailey's Tramroad between the Nantyglo Ironworks and a wharf on the Brecknock & Abergavenny Canal at Govilon. Here it met with the Llanvihangel Railway, a 3ft 6in line opened in 1811, which stretched for 6 ¼ miles to Llanvihangel Crucorney. There it joined with the Grosmont Railway, which opened in 1812, and the Hereford Railway opened in 1826. These tramroads were taken over by the Newport, Abergavenny & Hereford Railway (NA&HR) that was incorporated in 1846, although little progress seemed to have been made on further building of a railway until the opening of the section between Hereford and Pontypool in 1854.

In February 1859 Crawshay and his partner, Thomas Brown, acquired the Beaufort Tramroad that ran between Brynmawr and its junction with the Llanvihangel Railway at the canal wharf in Govilon. The next step for Bailey was to convert the tramways into a standard-gauge line connecting Merthyr, with its reserves of coal and iron ore, and Abergavenny, which was then in decline. Bailey was a lover of railways, which was hardly surprising, as it was the iron from his own works that was being used in their construction, but he was also described as being a 'promoter and sometimes turbulent director'.

To move his goods from the Nantyglo area the only line he could use at the time belonged to the Monmouthshire Railway & Canal Company that ran south via Aberbeeg and Risca through to Newport Docks. The MR&CC was incorporated in 1792 as the Monmouthshire Canal Company to construct canals from Newport to Crumlin and Pontnewynydd and associated 'rail ways', in essence 'tramroads'. The latter were soon found to be a more efficient means of transporting goods and later, passengers. Further acts authorised more tramroads, the use of locomotives, a change of name to the MR&CC in 1849 and later to convert those tramroads into railways. The costs of the latter coupled with a decline in trade and increasing competition from other railway companies finally resulted in amalgamation (in truth, a takeover) with the Great Western Railway, which became effective in 1880.

It is believed that Bailey fell out with the MR&CC due to what he thought were excessive track access charges and began thinking about connecting all the tramroads within his ownership to complete a line from Merthyr to Abergavenny. To gain access to his new line would require a new station at Abergavenny to connect the line to the NA&HR and running-rights would be required, as the NA&HR owned the existing line and infrastructure. This connection would allow access to the line north to Hereford and Shrewsbury and south to Newport and its docks via Pontypool Road as track access charges were apparently less than those being charged by the MR&CC.

The Merthyr, Tredegar & Abergavenny Railway, known locally as the 'Heads of the Valleys Line', was incorporated under an Act on 1st August 1859 with construction starting in June 1860. It wasn't too long before the railway became insolvent and was then leased to the London & North Western Railway for a period of 999 years on 8th November 1861. The Act confirming this was approved on 7th August 1862.

Our exploration of the line will begin at Abergavenny, as it was from here that the first section of the line to Brynmawr, then the highest station in Britain, was opened on 29th September 1862. This first section engineered by John Gardner involved eight bridges, two tunnels and a climb of over 1,000 feet, with one three-mile section demanding a rising gradient of 1 in 34, the steepest continuous ascent on Britain's railway network.

Abergavenny Junction opened on 1st October 1862, which was the first day of the LNWR lease of the line and the commencement of passenger services, although this lasted only until 20th June 1870, when the station was relocated 552 yards further north as the LNWR had sought to improve access to the Merthyr branch by remodelling the track layout.

A contract to build the line onward to Nantybwch was awarded in February 1862. This section of the line involved the construction of two viaducts and opened on 1st March 1864.

Further progress to Merthyr was opposed by the Brecon & Merthyr Railway, which had acquired the Old Rumney Railway from Rhymney to Bassaleg and had opened a line as far as Pant. The LNWR concluded an agreement with the Rhymney Railway in 1864 to jointly build the three miles of track from Nantybwch to Rhymney via Rhymney Bridge and give them running powers to Tyndall Street Goods Depot, Cardiff. This opened in September 1871. This was a shrewd move by the LNWR as before this date goods traffic had to pass through Newport, where the connecting GWR lines were still laid to Brunel's 7ft broad gauge up until 1872 when they and the remaining broad gauge lines in south Wales were finally relaid to standard gauge. This also effectively choked off the aspirations of the Brecon & Merthyr Railway to continue eastwards towards Abergavenny.

The MT&A reached Dowlais in 1873. To get from there to Merthyr the LNWR paid the B&M generous retrospective subsidies to allow it to have joint ownership of their line from Morlais to Cefn Coed, which opened in 1867 as part of its branch from Pontsticill Junction to Merthyr. This was eventually extended to Merthyr High Street station in 1868 through running powers granted by the GWR via a 44 chain link from Rhydycar Junction.

To establish a route into the town, the line curved around the west side to enter from the south. It extended for seven miles, descending on gradients of 1 in 50 or steeper, including two viaducts at Cefn Coed and Pontsarn, taking the track over the River Taff and one of its tributaries.

Cefn Coed viaduct, the third largest in Wales and now a Grade II listed structure, consisted of 15 arches, each one 39ft 6in wide, and is 770ft long, with a maximum height of 115ft. It was designed to be constructed entirely of limestone like the nearby Pontsarn viaduct but a strike by stonemasons in February 1866 caused the company to buy 800,000 bricks and use bricklayers to complete the 15 arches.

The final link which allowed MT&A trains to reach Merthyr from Abergavenny was the one-mile long section between Penywern Junction on the existing MT&A line near Dowlais, and Morlais Tunnel Junction on the now jointly owned B&M/

LNWR line to Merthyr. This opened in June 1879, allowing through trains to run over the whole length of the route between Abergavenny and Merthyr for the first time. A branch from Ebbw Vale Junction near Beaufort to Ebbw Vale was opened on 1st September 1867 and that from Tredegar to Nantybwch on 2nd November 1868.

Bailey's grandiose plans to connect the MT&A line to the north and south at Abergavenny Junction were not fully realised, as the LNWR wanted all freight to travel north over their metals so that they could benefit financially rather than some other company. Although a link to the south was apparently installed, there is no evidence that it was ever used, as Sir George Findlay, general manager of the LNWR, made a visit to the area and insisted that the link was removed, despite the fact that he was full of praise for the way in which the line had been substantially constructed. After the crossover was removed, the existing rails were left in situ truncated and according to the 1956 *Handbook of Stations* became holding sidings for a psychiatric hospital, a local merchant and the Wales Gas Board, but these had all closed by 1964.

Tredegar, once described as '...being the dirtiest and most unpleasant town in all the iron districts of South Wales', was connected to the MT&A by a northward extension of the line to Nantybwch. As well as providing passenger services this also opened a through route to Newport Docks via Nine Mile Point by a deal struck with the GWR, which gave access to the rich coal mining areas in the Sirhowy Valley under the powers of the Sirhowy Act of 1865.

South Wales was always predominantly the stronghold of the GWR, but both the LNWR and the Midland Railway also gained footholds to the south as far as Swansea through central Wales, the eastern Valleys to Blaenavon High Level and the north through arrangements with other companies.

The MT&A was yet another incursion of the LNWR into Wales, which already had sections of its line running south from Llanelli to Pontardulais. This was started in 1839 but was not finally completed as a through route from Shrewsbury to Swansea until 1871, with running powers granted through to Shrewsbury by the GWR from its junction with this route at Craven Arms. The GWR also granted running powers to the MT&A via the north-west route through Hereford. The LNWR was itself amalgamated into the London, Midland & Scottish Railway in 1923 and finally into British Railways ownership following nationalisation in 1948.

The LNWR ran through coaches from Cardiff Queen Street via Rhymney Bridge to Crewe, Liverpool, Manchester and, in summer, Blackpool. Through coaches also ran from Shrewsbury and Hereford to Merthyr. It wasn't too long before excursion traffic was introduced and on 11th July 1863, less than a year after the line was opened and being cognoscent of the old rallying cry of 'what about the workers', one Henry R. Marcus, a shipping agent from Liverpool who became known as 'the father of cheap trips', stepped forward. He became the originator of excursion trains and started advertising 'Marcus's Cheap Excursions', promising 'a grand trip for the working classes'. These ran across the MT&A to resorts along the north Wales coast and even to the Isle of Man.

Trains filled with race-goers travelled to Abergavenny races and to the markets and fairs that were frequently held there. Special trains also ran to Scotland filled with rugby fans to watch the international matches. A GPO sorting van used to run between London Euston and Merthyr via Stafford and Shrewsbury and the company's stationery stores van, which made deliveries to stations that had previously ordered supplies, ran on the first Monday in the month. This was usually attached to the rear of one of the morning passenger trains.

The station running-in boards along the route were styled in the typical hawkeye style used by the LNWR and the LMS. Some of which were described as 'formidable', informing passengers of the various junctions that connected to other lines along the route.

Operating rules on the line meant that the maximum speed allowed was a mere 30mph for passenger trains and only 20mph for freight, with passenger trains restricted to 25mph when descending downhill from Brynmawr to Abergavenny. The journey was time-consuming and slow as all coal trains were halted at periodic intervals to pin down the brakes on each wagon and then later for the release of their brakes. Nevertheless, coal traffic reached a peak in 1917 when 5,000 tons a day were despatched from the area.

Despite the speed restrictions, tight curves and other hazards, such as poor weather conditions, accidents were few and far between. On one memorable occasion, no fewer than 14 engines were snowed-in at various points across the line at Christmas 1927 and one train with forty passengers stuck over 1,100ft up in a snowdrift at Nantybwch. There were a number of recorded incidents, usually involving runaway coal trains, which was to be expected considering the many gradients. Fortunately, although rolling stock, not to mention a few buildings and structures, were considerably damaged, many of the train crews jumped clear before impact, so no serious injuries were reported.

The great depression in the 1930s that affected steelworks and collieries in south Wales, and indeed the whole of the country, meant a gradual decline in freight and passenger services. Following nationalisation in 1948 the newly-formed Western Region of British Railways took control of the MT&A and Sirhowy lines within their Newport Operating District and it was felt that it was more economical and practicable to route all freight traffic from the east of Abergavenny to Brynmawr, Ebbw Vale and Merthyr via Pontypool Road. This obviated the need to continue hauling freight loads up the 'great bank' from Abergavenny to Brynmawr. Regular freight traffic was therefore withdrawn from the MT&A route from 22nd November 1954 but passenger traffic continued until closure in 1958, thus providing the rare situation of a line continuing to be used for local passenger services after withdrawal of freight facilities, which was a complete reversal of the usual order.

In 1955 the Western Region of British Railways reorganised its passenger services and implemented them in the summer timetable. Due to falling passenger numbers on the line it had considered introducing diesel railcars as on other local services in Wales, such as the Newport to Usk and Monmouth branch via Little Mill. However, it was found that due to restricted clearances in some of the tunnels this was not feasible, and instead used 0-6-0 Pannier Tanks based at Merthyr shed hauling two-coach auto-trains. At this time the British Railways Modernisation Plan was still in its infancy and although the proposed introduction of diesel multiple unit numbers was to be greatly increased, the planned use of lightweight diesel railbuses for experimental use on rural services had yet to be implemented. If this had been the case it could be argued that their introduction onto the MT&A might have saved it for a few more

years at least, though it was very unlikely it would have survived the axe wielded by Dr Beeching a few years later.

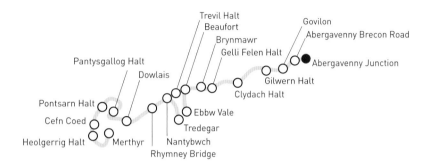

Our journey starts in Abergavenny, described in *Bradshaw's Handbook* of 1861 as an 'interesting old place and one where its present prosperity lies from flannel-weaving and the valuable coal and iron works at Clydach, Blaenavon and its neighbourhood, things that are likely to increase with the coming of the railways.'

Abergavenny Junction station was built on the GWR main line from Newport to Hereford to provide access to the MT&A. The main line, known as the North and West Route, is an important one, carrying freight as well as passenger trains.

This view is from the platform at Abergavenny Junction station where the ex-GWR line from Pontypool Road meets the ex-LNWR line from Merthyr. Arriving with the 5.15pm Cardiff General to Hereford is ex-GWR 4300 class 2-6-0 No 6352.

Ex-LMSR class 7F 0-8-0 No 49113 is seen with a southbound freight train at Abergavenny Junction station bound for the Newport area.

Ex-LMS class 2P No 41203 stands at Abergavenny Junction awaiting departure to Merthyr on 6th June 1953.

Two Crewe-built engines, 0-8-0s, G1 class No 49226 and G2A class No 49146, are seen leaving the branch with a trainload of ammonia tank wagons from the ICI works at Dowlais on 27th April 1954.

ABERGAVENNY

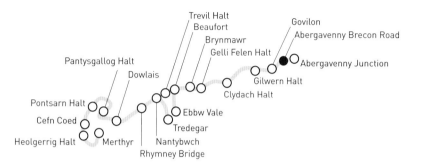

Trevil Halt
Beaufort
Brynmawr
Gelli Felen Halt
Govilon
Abergavenny Brecon Road
Abergavenny Junction
Pantysgallog Halt
Dowlais
Gilwern Halt
Clydach Halt
Pontsarn Halt
Cefn Coed
Ebbw Vale
Tredegar
Heolgerrig Halt
Merthyr
Nantybwch
Rhymney Bridge

On leaving Abergavenny Junction a short train ride brings us to Brecon Road Station, which is firmly within LNWR territory. The LNWR soon found that facilities for servicing locomotives at Abergavenny Junction were unsatisfactory and looked to providing proper arrangements at a different location. They chose a site close to the gasworks at Union Road to build a new locomotive shed, which was close to Brecon Road station. Construction started in 1867 and a turntable was provided in 1899 which lasted until 1953.

Right: Ex-LNWR Coal Tank No 27621 is about to leave Abergavenny (Brecon Road) with the 2.28pm service to Merthyr on 26th April 1948.

Abergavenny Union Road shed, code 86K, once housed over 100 locomotives.

The railway barracks used as sleeping quarters for train crews were also here and part of the infrastructure can still be seen. A plaque affixed to the boundary wall of the shed (below) commemorates the importance of this site.

This Plaque is to commemorate the railway people of Abergavenny

Abergavenny 1860

L M S

Merthyr 1960

Near this spot stood the local engine sheds which once housed nearly one hundred steam engines

The LNWR South Wales Engineer's coach and its locomotive, an elderly Allen 2-2-2 built at Crewe in 1852 which was given this role in 1911, is shown in the shed yard.

Left: An Abergavenny Union Road shed plate from the British Railways era when it was coded 86K.

On passing the locomotive shed on the right the line descended to cross the River Usk by a seven-span girder bridge and followed a circuitous route, skirting around the village of Llanfoist with the Blorenge Mountain on the left. It then began a 9-mile climb of about 1,000ft. with some gradients as steep as 1 in 38 to reach Govilon.

Ex-LMSR class 3 2-6-2T No 40145 is seen crossing the River Usk with a two-coach train from Abergavenny to Merthyr in September 1952.

GOVILON

Govilon station was opened on 1st October 1862 and originally had a staff of seven. This was where Crawshay Bailey built his three-storey stone warehouse, which still stands today, at the end of his tramroad to store iron alongside the Monmouthshire & Brecon Canal. On leaving the station there was a siding to the Wildon Iron Works. Govilon station once won an award for outstanding station gardens. It is now a private dwelling but retains some original features and is part of a cycleway.

GILWERN HALT

Our next station is Gilwern, where at one time there was a stone quarry and a siding, controlled from the signal box, but this was removed in 1921 following the closure of the quarry. Opened in 1863, Gilwern was downgraded to a halt in 1932 but was a busy little place in the summer months, as Sunday School children would alight here to spend the day picnicking alongside the Brecknock & Abergavenny Canal.

Here Ex-GWR 0-6-0 Pannier Tank No 6408 of 88D Merthyr shed brings a two-coach auto-train into Gilwern on an afternoon service to Merthyr.

CLYDACH HALT

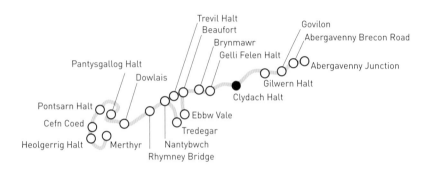

After Gilwern came Clydach, which was approached around a long, sweeping, graceful curve that carried the line over the Clydach viaduct high above the valley floor at a height of some 75ft.

This view from the platform at Clydach station shows ex-LMSR class 3F 0-6-0T No 47479 standing bunker-first at the head of a two-coach SLS Railtour on 14th July 1956. The enthusiasts have detrained to take photographs.

At the Merthyr end of Clydach station were the twin portals of Clydach tunnel. The station had two platforms and on the Up side toward Merthyr was the building that housed the ticket office and waiting room. This was a solid construction, built of limestone from the nearby quarry. The quarry and kilns supplied the adjacent Clydach Ironworks, where there were a number of private sidings.

This picture shows an unidentified 0-6-0 pannier tank, probably from Merthyr shed, on an auto-train working from Abergavenny rounding the curve as it climbs the Clydach Gorge with a service to Merthyr.

GELLI-FELEN HALT

The line was continuously rising and the firemen worked hard to maintain steam pressure on the approach to the twin tunnels at Gelli-Felen. The first tunnel opened in 1862 but in order to improve traffic flows a second tunnel was constructed in 1877. The picture shows an unidentified 0-6-0 Pannier Tank on a Merthyr to Abergavenny auto-train working leaving Gelli-Felen tunnel on 30th November 1957.

A small halt was built here with basic brick shelters. This view clearly shows its isolated location with the bare minimum of facilities. The halt, which opened in 1933 on a 1 in 38 gradient with staggered platforms, was built on a sweeping curve and was a favourite spot for derailments of the LNWR 0-8-4 tank locomotives which were used on the line, hence the laying of check rails on the curve.

BRYNMAWR

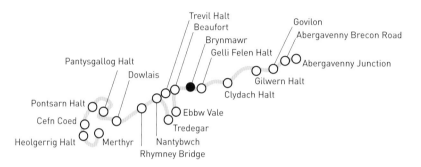

Trevil Halt
Beaufort
Brynmawr
Gelli Felen Halt
Govilon
Abergavenny Brecon Road
Abergavenny Junction
Pantysgallog Halt
Dowlais
Gilwern Halt
Clydach Halt
Pontsarn Halt
Cefn Coed
Ebbw Vale
Heolgerrig Halt
Merthyr
Tredegar
Nantybwch
Rhymney Bridge

A mile or so further on we arrive at Brynmawr. There was plenty to see here as this was a meeting point for a number of lines. Brynmawr opened on 1st October 1862 and was the junction for lines to Blaenavon High Level, the Western Valley line to Newport via Nantyglo and Aberbeeg and Ebbw Vale High Level. It is ironic that it was 100 years from first opening to the final closure of Brynmawr on 30th April 1962. Once described as having 'something of a Wild West air' due to its location at 1200ft above sea level, for a time it was Britain's highest station. To the south of the station, which had seven platforms, there were extensive sidings and a turntable.

The first services to be withdrawn were the ones to Pontypool via Blaenavon High Level in 1941, followed by those on the Ebbw Vale branch on 2nd April 1951. The Western Valley line to Newport via Aberbeeg clung on into the 1960s and some attempt was made to enhance services by the introduction of diesel multiple units operating a fairly frequent service prior to total closure. Here ex-GWR 6400 class 0-6-0 Pannier Tank No 6427 leaves Brynmawr with a Merthyr to Abergavenny train on 2nd January 1958, just three days prior to the closure of the line.

Three days later, on 5th January 1958, the last train from Abergavenny is shown standing at Brynmawr awaiting departure for Merthyr.

BEAUFORT

Eleven miles after leaving Abergavenny the line arrived at Beaufort, which opened on 1st March 1864; much of the surrounding land was originally owned by the Duke of Beaufort. In 1867 a branch to Ebbw Vale was opened with trains running through from Brynmawr, a station once served by over 30 trains a day. Trains for Ebbw Vale had to pass over both the Beaufort and Rhyd-y-Blew viaducts. The line to Ebbw Vale closed in 1951. There was once an ironworks and brickworks located here that produced a very hard engineering brick, and it is alleged that these formed the foundations for the Empire State Building in New York City.

As this photograph shows, weather conditions at Beaufort could be very harsh in winter.

A passenger train hauled by an unidentified Webb-designed 0-6-2 Coal Tank crosses Beaufort viaduct on the Ebbw Vale branch.

EBBW VALE

At Ebbw Vale Junction a line swung left down into Ebbw Vale High Level, which was the terminus of the LNWR branch line. The other station at Ebbw Vale belonged to the GWR. The High Level station, although more centrally located in the town than the Low Level GWR station, had the disadvantage that its services only went as far as Brynmawr, whilst its rival's went through to Newport.

Ex-LNWR Coal Tank, bearing its BR number 58916 is shown at Ebbw Vale High Level running bunker-first on a service for Brynmawr on 19th August 1950.

TREVIL HALT

Back on the main line, the halfway point was reached at Trevil approximately twelve miles from Abergavenny Junction. The station was in an isolated spot, although it had a long association with tramroads, the first having been built in 1793. There were private sidings to the Beaufort Ironworks but these were closed in 1938 at the same time that the signal box was replaced by a frame in the bay window of the station house in order to maintain its function as a block post. In 1932 the station was downgraded to a halt.

NANTYBWCH

Crossing the nine-arch Blaen-y-Cwm Viaduct, now a Grade II listed monument, the line entered Nantybwch, an important junction where the line from Abergavenny connected with the Sirhowy Railway.

The original Sirhowy Tramway had been authorised as far back as 1802. It changed its name to the Sirhowy Railway under an Act of Parliament in 1860 and was then taken over by the LNWR in 1876. The line ran south to meet what became the Great Western line to Newport at Nine Mile Point, thus providing the MT&A with potential access to traffic from the myriad of collieries along that route.

The Sirhowy line was extended north to meet the MT&A in 1868. The place where it joined the line had originally been rather optimistically named Tredegar but this was renamed Nantybwch in 1868, there being a station already in the heart of Tredegar on the Sirhowy line.

Situated some 1,165ft above sea level, Nantybwch was a bleak and isolated spot, especially in winter, when snow blizzards could obliterate the landscape.

When services on the Sirhowy Valley line were withdrawn, on 13th June 1960, this marked the end for Nantybwch, trains on the line from Abergavenny to Merthyr having been withdrawn two years earlier.

Right: On the 19th August 1950 an ex-LNWR 0-6-2 tank bearing its recently acquired British Railways No 58891 stands at Nantybwch station on a stopping train for Abergavenny Junction.

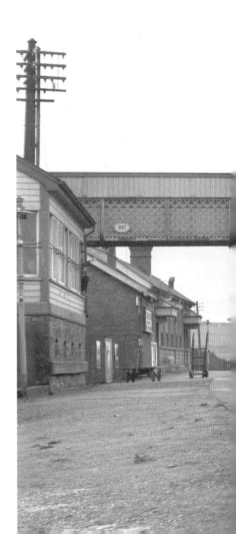

Ex-GWR 0-6-0 Pannier Tank No 6426 of 86A Newport (Ebbw Junction) shed simmers gently in the sunshine at Nantybwch with a single-coach auto-train, having just arrived from Abergavenny in 1958.

The branch from Tredegar to Nantybwch opened on 2nd November 1868. A former LNWR coal tank of 86K Abergavenny shed is seen at Tredegar with a local train, still in LMS livery but bearing its new BR number, 58921.

There was a four-road engine shed at Tredegar that was a sub-shed of Abergavenny.

RHYMNEY BRIDGE

Rhymney Bridge station, like many others on this line, was situated in a desolate location, although this was an important junction that had offered connections to Cardiff and Newport. Services on the Rhymney branch had ceased on 23rd September 1953 and goods facilities were withdrawn from Rhymney Bridge on 22nd November 1954.

Rhymney Bridge must surely have rarely ever been as busy as it was for the arrival there of the valedictory railtour the day after public services had ended.

DOWLAIS

Such was the importance attached to it that Dowlais boasted no fewer than five railway stations, owned and operated by a number of different companies. The combination of locally available coal, limestone and iron ore together with an abundance of water was to make this desolate part of south Wales ripe for the development of an industry that would soon embrace the world, namely the iron industry. The Dowlais Iron Company would become the largest in the world, the first to use the process of converting iron into steel by the new invention of the Bessemer Converter. The first Dowlais station on the MT&A opened in 1873 and was called Dowlais Top, a name it shared with the nearby station on the B&M line. This first station was closed in 1885 and replaced from 4th May of that year by a new one called Dowlais High Street, closer to the centre of the town.

Ex-GWR 0-6-0 Pannier Tank No 6423 arrives at Dowlais High Street with the 11.08am service to Merthyr from Abergavenny on 7th September 1957.

PANTYSGALLOG HALT

An unidentified LNWR Coal Tank 0-6-2T is seen at Pantysgallog with a stopping train. This was another wind-swept, isolated location when first built but urban expansion brought it closer to the town. The Brecon & Merthyr Railway also had a station here and to distinguish between the two the suffix Low Level was added to the MT&A station in 1950. The platforms came into use on 2nd February 1914 and were very basic, made from timber and surfaced with ash.

Just beyond Pantysgallog Halt the line entered the double-track Morlais tunnel, which marked the start of the descent toward Merthyr. An LNWR Coal Tank 0-6-2T No 3017 is shown running bunker-first at Morlais Junction with a train of empty coal wagons heading toward Merthyr.

PONTSARN HALT

Pontsarn Looking East No. 37.11.

During the summer months Pontsarn could be a very busy place where many thousands of passengers from chapels and Sunday Schools would alight to attend their annual outings in the adjacent fields. The station was redesignated as a halt in June 1953.

The picture shows GWR ex Taff Vale Railway M1 class 0-6-2T No 482, built in 1891 and withdrawn in 1927, crossing the seven-arch Pontsarn viaduct with a passenger train.

CEFN COED

The fifteen-arch Cefn Coed viaduct, still standing today as a listed monument, was once described by the Cefn Coed stationmaster as 'simplicity, magnificence and perfection of proportions'. He wasn't wrong. An unidentified ex-GWR 0-6-0 Pannier Tank propels its two-coach auto-train into Cefn Coed station having just crossed the viaduct.

HEOLGERRIG HALT

An additional stopping place, the wind-swept and isolated Heolgerrig Halt on this last stretch of the line close to Merthyr, was opened on 31st May 1937.

MERTHYR

An hour and a half after departing from Abergavenny and having covered 24 ½ miles, the train finally arrived at Merthyr. Six different railway companies ran services from here to all parts of the country, reflecting its status at the time as one of the largest and most prosperous towns in Wales. The original station roof was designed by Isambard Kingdom Brunel using the same type of circular roof beams he had employed at London Paddington.

The first station at Merthyr was opened by the Taff Vale Railway on 21st April 1841 at Plymouth Street. High Street station opened in 1853 and this picture, taken around 1909, gives a panoramic view of the station with a GWR 2021 class 0-6-0ST No 2069 taking water from a typical GWR conical tank water column. In the background is the train shed, with the substantial granary shed in the right middle ground.

This picture of Merthyr station taken in August 1951 shows an ex-GWR 0-6-0T 5691 on the left whilst on the right is ex-GWR PT's 6434 on an auto service to Dowlais and 6437 on a train to Pontsticill Junction.

Merthyr had its own locomotive shed, coded 88D, that provided motive power for a wide range of duties, but this closed in 1964.

The picture opposite of Merthyr shed was taken in 1955 and shows on the left one of the Ivatt-designed 2-6-2 tank engines sometimes used on the line to Abergavenny as well as a number of ex-GWR Pannier Tanks, the workhorses of the former Great Western lines in south Wales.

The day after public services ended on 5th February 1958, a special train organised by the Stephenson Locomotive Society ran the whole length of the line from Abergavenny to Merthyr hauled by a pair of ex-LNWR locomotives. The train was headed by G2 class 0-8-0 No 49121, piloted by 0-6-2 Coal Tank No 58926. No 49121 entered service in June 1910 and lasted over 48 years until withdrawal on 30th September 1958. The other loco, No 58926, a Webb 0-6-2 Coal Tank, was built at Crewe and entered service in September 1888, during the reign of Queen Victoria. This remarkable engine served for over 70 years before withdrawal in October 1958. Fortunately, it survived the cutter's torch and now operates on the Keighley & Worth Valley Railway, which was the setting for the film *The Railway Children*.

Today the station at Merthyr is but a shadow of its former self, with the new franchise operator, KeolisAmey, providing a half-hourly service to the coastal resorts of south Wales and beyond via Cardiff. The station layout at Merthyr was radically altered in recent years and now it has just one platform, with the whole of the surrounding area now covered by retail outlets, yet it still boasts over half a million passengers annually.

This picture shows Class 150 Sprinter 150242 awaiting departure from Merthyr on the 4.08pm service to Barry Island on 6th June 2018.

CREDITS

Lost Lines of Wales – The Heads of the Valleys Line. Published in Great Britain in 2018 by Graffeg Limited.

Written by Geoffrey Charles Lloyd copyright © 2018. Designed and produced by Graffeg Limited copyright © 2018.

Graffeg Limited, 24 Stradey Park Business Centre, Mwrwg Road, Llangennech, Llanelli, Carmarthenshire, SA14 8YP, Wales, UK. Tel 01554 824000. www.graffeg.com.

Geoffrey Charles Lloyd is hereby identified as the author of this work in accordance with section 77 of the Copyrights, Designs and Patents Act 1988.

A CIP Catalogue record for this book is available from the British Library.

ISBN 9781912654154

1 2 3 4 5 6 7 8 9

Photo credits

© J Wood/Kidderminster Railway Museum: pages 14, 30. © P M Alexander/Kidderminster Railway Museum: pages 16, 26. © P B Whitehouse/Kidderminster Railway Museum: pages 42, 45. © R J Leonard/Kidderminster Railway Museum: pages 37. © W H Smith collection/Kidderminster Railway Museum: pages 51, 55. © G M Perkins/Kidderminster Railway Museum: page 58. © A Donaldson/Kidderminster Railway Museum: page 61. © V R Webster/Kidderminster Railway Museum: page 53. © Stan Brown Collection: pages 17, 18, 24, 46. © SLS Collection: pages 21, 29, 62. © Gerald Davies Collection: pages 22, 28, 34, 41, 49, 54. © Tom Watkins: page 32. © Rev. Bob Jones /Online Transport Archive: pages 33, 56. © Michael Hale/Great Western Trust: page 35. © I .Wright: page 39. © Seabourne Collection: page 40. © Rev. Christopher Gwilliam: page 43. © W A Camwell/GD Collection: pages 47, 48. © Alan George, 'Old Merthyr Tydfil' www.alangeorge.co.uk: page 50. © P. J. Garland Collection per R. S. Carpenter: page 57. © Laurence Waters/Great Western Trust: page 59. © Geoffrey Charles Lloyd: pages 23, 25, 60, 63.

The photographs used in this book have come from a variety of sources. Wherever possible contributors have been identified although some images may have been used without credit or acknowledgement and if this is the case apologies are offered and full credit will be given in any future edition.

Cover: Clydach Gorge

Back cover: Abergavenny, Tredegar, Merthyr.

Titles in the Lost Lines of Wales series:

Cambrian Coast Line
ISBN 9781909823204

Aberystwyth to Carmarthen
ISBN 9781909823198

Brecon to Newport
ISBN 9781909823181

Ruabon to Barmouth
ISBN 9781909823174

Chester to Holyhead
ISBN 9781912050697

Shrewsbury to Aberystwyth
ISBN 9781912050680

The Mid Wales Line
ISBN 9781912050673

Vale of Neath
ISBN 9781912050666

Rhyl to Corwen
ISBN 9781912213108

The Heads of the Valleys Line
ISBN 9781912654154

Conwy Valley Line
ISBN 9781912654147